A Beautiful Struggle
When Trials Become Trophies

Daiheem Kearse

Unless otherwise noted, all Scripture quotations are from the King James Version of the Bible.

A Beautiful Struggle
When Trials Become Trophies
ISBN 978-0967951669

Copyright ©2018 by Daiheem Kearse

Published by
Full Effect Gospel Ministries, Inc.
Brooklyn, NY

Printed in the United States of America.
This book or parts thereof may not be reproduced in any form, stored in a retrieval system, or transmitted in any form by any means – electronic, mechanical, photocopy, recording or otherwise- without prior written permission of the publisher, except as provided by the United States of America copyright law.

This book is available at special quantity discounts for bulk purchase for sales promotions, fund-raising and educational needs. For information please write fulleffectmail@aol.com.

Edited by The Full Effect Editing Team
 Wanza Leftwich, The Gospel Writer www.wanzaleftwich.com
 Cynthia McInnis, Author, Biblical Educator, Expositor

DEDICATION

To my children,
Judah Daiheem, Trinity Jael,
Zion Travis and Gabriel Oliver

I love you to life.
You are the reason I never gave up.
Daddy will always love you!

ACKNOWLEDGMENTS

Special thanks to

My Parents,

Willie James Kearse and Linda Stallings, Thank you for praying for me all night on the altar when I was an infant.

My Wife,

Alicia Kearse, Thank you for pushing me to do things that I never thought possible. I love you.

My Children,

Judah Daiheem, Trinity Jael, Zion Travis and Gabriel Oliver.

I love you very much.

My Bishop,

Archie L. McInnis, II

Thank you for seeing greatness in me when no one else did. I appreciate you because you never gave up on me even when I was in the struggle.

This book would not be possible without the assistance of my beautiful First Lady, Dr. Cynthia McInnis and the wonderful Elder Wanza Leftwich. To my Full Effect Gospel Ministries family, I love you all.

FOREWORD

"Though he were a Son, yet learned he obedience by the things which he suffered;"
Hebrews 5:8 KJV.

"Yet He (Jesus) learned His obedience, not from His Sonship, but from His sufferings. As the Son, He was always obedient to the Father's will; but the special obedience needed to qualify Him as our High Priest, He learned experimentally in practical suffering" (Commentary Critical and Explanatory on the Whole Bible).

Daiheem Kearse's revelation of "A Beautiful Struggle " is a sound and profound discovery of self-awareness. To be able to see your struggles and trials working together for your good is a God insight. When you can see that there is better for you in your future, you won't settle with your present. I've seen this young man go from bad to worse and yet he remained faithful to ministry. As his Pastor and spiritual father I wanted to help him as I would help my very own children. Even though I did help him grow and mature as much as I could, there were some things that he had to endure on his own.

There are some things we must learn and endure without the help of others to fulfill God's purpose in life. The scripture says that Jesus learned obedience through the things that he suffered. As a son, Jesus never disobeyed his Father's will. But in order to become qualified to be our High Priest he had to experience and endure a level of suffering without the Father's help. The scholars call it "Special Obedience." Jesus did what no one else was willing to do. The beautiful thing about this is that without his suffering his purpose would not have been fulfilled. His purpose was to bring salvation to the world. The sufferings of Jesus and his crucifixion were a heinous crime but became a beautiful victory and brought salvation to those that believe in his name.

"But he was wounded for our transgressions, he was bruised for our iniquities: the chastisement of our peace was upon him; and with his stripes we are healed." Isaiah 53:5. Jesus' struggle became our victory!

So many want so much but are not willing to pay the price for what they want. We discard our dreams and desires when the contrary winds of life blow against us. Instead of quitting, have you considered that maybe your trial or problem can be the thing that brings the winner out of you? Maybe that struggle is the thing that is designed to show you what problems you were put on this earth to solve. If you can see your struggles that way then, it's "A Beautiful Struggle."

Pastor Kearse has earned the right to be heard. He has a voice of victory and a fresh word from the Lord. Through his pain, he has remained faithful to God and to the work of his hands. He is a Joseph to Pharaoh, a Joshua to Moses, a Timothy to Paul, a true follower of Christ, and my spiritual son of who I am Godly proud.

Daiheem has proven, through test and trial, that if you remain faithful to God with all your heart, you'll see mountains become mole hills, pain become gain and trials become trophies. I agree that Daiheem Kearse has experienced "A Beautiful Struggle." I've seen God raise him up from the ashes to the mighty man of God that he is today. Read, *A Beautiful Struggle,* and it will help you discover your own beauty in the making.

Bishop Archie L. McInnis, II
BALM2
Senior Pastor & Founder,
Full Effect Gospel Ministries, Inc.
Headquarters, Brooklyn, New York

Table of Contents

Chapter		Page
One	*In Pursuit of Promise*	1
Two	*Not My Fault But It Is My Challenge*	11
Three	*Connections Are Everything*	20
Four	*Worshiping In It*	32
Five	*Dig Ditches*	43
Six	*Results After Offering*	53
Seven	*Not Just Water*	62

A Beautiful Struggle
In Pursuit of Promise

CHAPTER ONE
In Pursuit of Promise

As a young boy, it was instilled in me that when someone made a promise to you, it was guaranteed to happen. When my parents said that they were going to give me something, I was happy about it. I became more excited about it when they said, "We promise!"

When a promise is made it is supposed to be kept. In life, people make many promises to themselves and to others. However, it is interesting to note that not all of these promises are kept. From marriage to parenting, to business deals, whether it is a spoken or unspoken promise, a promise is a promise and it is not meant to be broken.

In 2 Kings 3:4-7, the king of Moab rebelled against Israel. He stopped giving Israel what was promised to them because King Ahab died. In response to the king of Moab's rebellious action, King Jehoram made a choice to go after what was promised to them. I found out that just because a promise might not be kept, it does not mean you can't pursue it. It's yours to pursue.

    Have you ever been in a position where someone reneged on what they said or something happened that they were unable to keep their word? Life, in itself, has ups and downs and things don't always go according to plan. Could it be a father not being in the household or disobedient children that do what they want to do? Perhaps your employer says, "We're going to give you a raise," but doesn't and now you're in a financial dilemma. How about your body becomes sick out of nowhere, and you have afflictions from all angles? Even in all of this, a choice has to be made. Do we give up on what we believe belongs to us or do we pursue?

    It is easy to give up. Giving up takes no effort, it takes no thought, and it's very easy to do. But there is never a reward in giving up. To give up or to quit is to say that the promise is not worth it. It says that your kid's success is not worth it, it says your marriage is not worth it. Giving up and quitting is exactly what the enemy wants you to do. The enemy doesn't want you to pursue your promise because he understands the power in *obtaining*.

Matthew 13:12 says, "For whosoever hath, to him shall be given, and he shall have more abundance: but whosoever hath not, from him shall be taken away even that he hath." What does this mean? The more you go after what you want the more what you want will come to you. The more you try to obtain, the more you will increase and the more you increase, the more influence you will have.

Influence produces fellowship. I'm not just talking about material things but I speak of the whole spectrum of our existence; mental, physical, and spiritual. The more you increase in all of these areas, the easier it becomes to gain influence with people. One thing the devil does not want is for a Christian to increase! He does not want you to have influence.

Many people follow rappers, singers, great political figures, athletes, and television stars because they have obtained the things that drew their interest. These influential people pursued their dreams. They went after their goals and they increased. I'm quite sure that in their pursuit, they ran into obstacles and various situations that arose but because you see their results, you understand that they did not stop.

As children of God, we have the right to be blessed. We have the right to prosper. We have the right to pursue what was promised to us. We have the right to conquer and get what is ours, but many times we stop in mid-pursuit because of difficulties or unexpected events. No matter the obstacles we have to endure, we have to keep working and keep pursuing.

We can't change our minds about what we want because of the work and effort we have to put in. Anybody that has ever been successful and is maintaining success has to put in some work and effort. Without it, you won't be able to accomplish anything. "Wealth obtained by fraud dwindles, but the one who gathers by labor increases it." Proverb 13:11NASB

I believe the lack of work and effort will cause decay. When something is not being used or worked on it tends to rust or die. Whether it's a building, a person, a

A Beautiful Struggle
In Pursuit of Promise

---

dream or promise, it is imperative that you don't let your dreams die. Don't let the promise die, and don't change your mind. You have the ability to accomplish whatever you put your mind to. God has given us the power to think and he wants us to think good thoughts.

Philippians 4:8 says, "Finally, brethren, whatsoever things are true, whatsoever things are honest, whatsoever things are just, whatsoever things are pure, whatsoever things are lovely, whatsoever things are of good report; if there be any virtue, and if there be any praise, think on these things." Be careful how you think when it comes to pursuing your promise because your bad thoughts can paralyze your progress. How you think matters!

Jehoram made a decision to go after what was his. He gathered the people together to pursue the promise but in the midst of the pursuit they came to a point where they lacked water (2 Kings 3:9). There are times when you can prepare and be in a position to believe everything is well until you are in the midst of pursuit and you realize that something is lacking.

A Beautiful Struggle
In Pursuit of Promise

    For example, we pursue our promise so that our families can be well off and enjoy life but yet our children don't want to listen and they want to act as if we didn't raise them the right way. We pursue a good marriage and we can't seem to please our spouse and we tried everything but yet nothing is working. We pursue financial freedom but yet the business can't seem to get off the ground; we can't find a job, we are robbing Peter to pay Paul and our financial situation is in the forefront of our lives while we can't get what we need or even what we want. We are doing everything in our power to stay healthy. We eat right, we take vitamins, we exercise and yet the doctor's report says that we have cancer, heart disease or some kind of sickness. All of these examples, and believe me, there are plenty more, all represent LACK OF WATER. Anything that's missing, anything that's broken, anything that comes to hinder your pursuit of promise, is a lack of water. Now the huge question is, do you stop pursuing the promise or do you pursue in spite of the lack? The answer is to pursue in spite of!

A Beautiful Struggle
In Pursuit of Promise

King David was in a position where he had to decide whether to stop or whether to pursue. The Bible says that King David, his family and the wives of his soldiers were taken captive and their city was burned down with fire. (2 Kings 30)

Can you imagine someone taking your spouse and children and then burning down your house? Is that enough to stop you from pursuing? David didn't respond with an, *"I quit"*, attitude even though he may have felt like it. The Bible says he encouraged himself and he inquired of the Lord. In other words, he prayed. The Lord told him to pursue for you shall surely overtake them, and without fail recover all. This right here gives us two specific actions we must take when we are faced with a situation that comes to hinder our pursuit.

The first one is to encourage yourself. You should speak good things into the atmosphere for you and about you. Focus on victory not defeat and think about how God did it before and declare that he will do it again. Surround yourself with people that are like-minded; that will speak life into your situation and not death. Listen to faith-based music and audio podcasts, read your word and speak the word. Write down the Scriptures of faith and victory and post them up in your room, on your refrigerator, and on your wall so you can be reminded to keep moving and pursuing.

The second is to inquire of God, which simply, for me means to pray. Prayer is very essential in this journey we call life. Prayer is communication with God. It is a time of asking of God and receiving from God. It is also an exercise of faith knowing and believing that God hears and answers according to His good will and love for us. In the scripture we are commanded to pray.

Matthew 5:44 "…pray for them which despitefully use you, and persecute you."

Mark 13:33 "Take ye heed, watch and pray…"

Luke 18:1 "And he spake a parable unto them to this end, that men ought always to pray, and not to faint."

Ephesians 6:18 "Praying always with all prayer and supplication in the Spirit…"

Rom 12:12 "Rejoicing in hope; patient in tribulation; continuing instant in prayer."

Colossians 4:2 "Continue in prayer..."

1 Thessalonians 5:17 "Pray without ceasing."

1 Timothy 2:8 "I will therefore that men pray every where, lifting up holy hands, without wrath and doubting."

When we respond to God's command to pray we will notice that we become closer to him and things begin to happen. "Ask, and it shall be given you; seek, and ye shall find; knock, and it shall be opened unto you: For every one that asketh receiveth; and he that seeketh findeth; and to him that knocketh it shall be opened." Matthew 7:7-11

Prayer will help you conquer any and everything that you will ever come up against because there is power in prayer. The power in prayer is not a power that comes from the act of prayer. It is a power that flows from the one we are praying to. We, as human beings, are blessed to be able to reach up to God in prayer knowing that He hears us. In his omnipotence, he responds and we receive. That's the power of prayer! Prayer unleashes a deeper relationship with God in our hearts and it comforts our souls. It develops a stronger faith in which he unleashes power in us to live our lives in service to him and others. The power is not in our petition. The power comes from his response and a confidence in knowing He is ever present with us.

You have to encourage yourself, pray, act on what God says and then watch God move on your behalf, in the midst of your pursuit of promise. David prayed to the Lord. God answered David and told him to pursue. David recovered all from his enemies. He obtained everything he went after. Pursuing the promise does not have to end with defeat. It can end beautifully, just like it did for David.

CHAPTER TWO
Not My Fault But It Is My Challenge

"Why is this happening to me?" is a question I've asked God many times trying to figure out what I had done to deserve these storms, trials, and trouble. In life, there are many times when we try to pinpoint the reason we go through what we go through. We tend to put this heavy weight on our shoulders and say, "I deserve this because of what I've done."

I want to help you. Most of the things that we deal with are not our fault. We can go all the way back to Adam and Eve. They ate from the Tree of Good and Evil that the Lord told Adam not to eat from and we deal with the consequences of his actions until this day (Genesis 3:14-19). It's not your fault that you have to deal with the consequences of Adams actions, just like it's not your fault that you were raised in a single-parent home or in foster care. It's not your fault you were raped or molested. It's not your fault that you have a hereditary

A Beautiful Struggle
Not My Fault But It Is My Challenge

sickness. But in all of these circumstances, it is your challenge.

When you see what you go through as a challenge it changes your view of it. You look for ways to overcome it rather than looking for someone or something to blame.

In 2 Kings 3, King Jehoram, two other kings, a host of men and cattle ventured out on a journey to Moab to possess what was rightfully theirs because the king of Moab broke the promise that was made to Israel. While on that journey they ran into a problem, they had no water. Immediately King Jehoram began to speak blame and the language of defeat.

2 Kings 3:10 says, "And the king of Israel said, Alas! that the Lord hath called these three kings together, to deliver them into the hand of Moab!" He blamed the Lord for bringing them together and then leaving them stranded with no water. But when you read 2 Kings 3:6-7 you will see that it was Jehoram that brought the kings together and wanted to go against Moab. Don't get me wrong, Jehoram had a right to pursue but not to blame.

A Beautiful Struggle
Not My Fault But It Is My Challenge

Blaming yourself and others will put you in the mindset of defeat.

Adam blamed Eve. "And the man said, The woman whom thou gavest to be with me, she gave me of the tree, and I did eat." Genesis 3:12

See, some believe that finding fault and blame will shift the weight of the situation to the one or the thing that is being blamed. But the truth is, you still have to deal with the situation no matter whose fault it is, no matter who is to blame. If you are going through a storm or trouble that seems unbearable you have to understand that it is just a season and it will pass. If you are seeking a way out you must do it without blame.

Seeking a way out is to seek God, not blame him. Jehoshaphat, one of the kings who was with Jehoram, had a different outlook on the situation. He wanted to seek the Lord for a solution. "But Jehoshaphat said, Is there not here a prophet of the Lord , that we may enquire of the Lord by him?" (2 Kings 3:11) Whenever you are facing challenges or great turmoil in your life the first person you should reach out to is the Lord. He's the one with all the answers.

In life we are faced with numerous obstacles. Some of them we caused but some had nothing to do with us. For instance, where you grew up, the family that you have and the things you were exposed to as a young child. All of these situations were out of your control and if they were bad situations it wasn't your fault that they were bad. You never asked to be in them in the first place, but just because you didn't ask to be in them it does not mean you're not faced with the challenges of them.

There is no doubt that challenges will come. No one is exempt from storms or trouble or trials. The Bible says that man that is born of a woman is of few days, and full of trouble. Job 14:1

How we handle our challenges determine whether we win or lose. There are times you have to lose some things to win. It is possible to lose some stuff and still win. Let's take Job's life as an example. He was wealthy, blameless and upright, always careful to avoid

A Beautiful Struggle
Not My Fault But It Is My Challenge

doing evil. He was righteous in the sight of God but that did not exclude him from trouble, trials and tragedies. Job's name was brought up in a conversation with God and Satan. The outcome of that conversation resulted in Job losing everything he had. In the course of one day, Job received four messages, each bearing separate news that his livestock, servants, and ten children had all died at the hands of murdering invaders or by natural disasters. Job tore his clothes and shaved his head in mourning, but he still blessed God in his prayers.

Job was afflicted with horrible skin sores. His wife encouraged him to curse God and to give up and die, but Job refused. Job's three friends tried to help the situation by sharing their thoughts about his afflictions. The premise of the friends' argument was that misfortune only follows evil deeds, but Job wasn't evil. See, Job and his friends were trying to explain the nature of God with only the limited information available to human knowledge, as God himself noted when he roared from the whirlwind, "Who is this that darkness counsel by words without knowledge?" Job 38:2

A Beautiful Struggle
Not My Fault But It Is My Challenge

We have no clue what God has planned for us. We will never fully understand God's reason for doing things. It has to be revealed to us. See, we know why Job went through all of this because we read it and the word tells us it was God who instigated it. (Job 1:8; 2:3) but Job didn't understand why he was going through all of this. His friends didn't know neither did his wife. No one knew why these things were happening to Job but he had to endure it. Only God and Satan knew. God trusted Job with trouble; God knew that job would not curse him nor turn his back on him. This is what many of us are dealing with today; God has entrusted us with trouble. We have been considered and in the end we will be rewarded.

It wasn't Job's fault that he had to deal with all of these situations; he didn't do anything to deserve such pain. He lost his children, his wife turned on him, sick in his body and his friends couldn't help him. All these things had to be endured. In the end Job was restored. He was given double for his trouble. Everything he lost, he got back and so much more. Job 42:10

A Beautiful Struggle
Not My Fault But It Is My Challenge

He faced his challenges head-on and in return he received his reward. We have to face our challenges head-on. We have to go against the mindset of giving up. We have to keep the word of God on our minds even at the lowest and toughest point of our lives. We cannot accept defeat. We can't look to blame someone or something; instead we must focus on a solution.

There is nothing new under the sun. There may be new methods but it is the same message. Everything that takes place today, God knows about it. So why not go to his word to understand how to take on the challenges of life. Believe me it's in the word. It is better to go to the word of God than to assume we know how to handle challenges on our own.

When there is a lack of understanding we start to assume then we make our decisions based on our assumption, not on truth. You would be surprised at how many people gave up because of their assumptions. We assume that Christ doesn't want anything to do with us because of what we've done so we leave church and don't come back. We assume things won't get better so instead of moving forward we stay where we are and reminisce on past victories.

The assumptions that we have will cause us to abort our destiny. That is why we must get an understanding of the word. It is so important. The Bible says study to show thyself approved. 2 Timothy 2:15. It also says in 2 Timothy 3:16-17also says, "All scripture is given by inspiration of God, and is profitable for doctrine, for reproof, for correction, for instruction in righteousness: That the man of God may be perfect, thoroughly furnished unto all good works."

Studying the word of God will give you an understanding of God's mind and God's will for your life. When you know that he will never leave you nor forsake you, you will have confidence in knowing that he loves you in spite of everything you've done and he loves you where you are right now. His word will guide you. Psalm 119:105 says, "Your word is a lamp to my feet and a light to my path." If we read and heed the Lord's instructions he will show us where to go, what to say, and how to make decisions. His Word also reveals

A Beautiful Struggle
Not My Fault But It Is My Challenge

when we're heading in the wrong direction and warns us of the consequences of continuing down that path.

Be encouraged to know that although trials will come into your life, don't give up. It may not be your fault but God can certainly help you overcome the challenges that you face and turn those trials into trophies.

CHAPTER THREE

Connections Are Everything

The world has never been more connected. Companies and individuals have made billions of dollars creating ways for people to connect around the world. Never in history has there been a time when you can be in one place and still connect with people around the world via text message, Face Time, Face book, Twitter, Instagram, etc.

This clearly lets me know that making connections is important. The only other thing that might be more important than a simple connection is who you're connected to.

"Be careful of the company you keep."

"Your friends are your future self."

These are quotes that we often hear when we speak about making connections. When we look at it from a biblical perspective, we understand that there are many scriptures that mention whom we should be connected to.

A Beautiful Struggle
Connections Are Everything

"Whoever keeps company with the wise becomes wise, but the companion of fools suffers harm." Proverbs 13:20, ISV

"As iron sharpens iron, so a friend sharpens a friend:" Proverbs 27:17, ESV

"Don't hang out with angry people; don't keep company with hotheads. Bad temper is contagious – don't get infected." Proverbs 22:24-25, MSG

These scriptures explain the importance of your connections. Whether friend or relative, your connection is very important. It can determine the outcome of your situation.

In 2 Kings 3:9-14, Kings Jehoram, Jehoshaphat, and the king of Edom found themselves in a place of need. They needed water for themselves and for everyone that was with them. Jehoram's first response was to blame God, but it is a good thing he was connected to Jehoshaphat because Jehoshaphat's first response was to seek God for a solution. When you are connected to people, they have the ability to cause you to think and act differently.

A Beautiful Struggle
Connections Are Everything

Instead of blaming God, let's seek God. Your surrounding should not comprise of people who think and act just like you. Our differences are what makes us special! We cannot be afraid to connect with those who think differently or who were raised differently than we were, even those that are of different ethnicity. We need to connect with those who are smarter than we are and have more wisdom than we do. Pay attention and seek out people who not only know more but are willing to challenge and push you. It's easy to get lost in your ideas because few things are as important as gaining new perspectives. Alternate perspectives can eliminate the blind spots and bring you down from the mindset that says, "I know it all".

Now, connection is also twofold. It can help you out of a situation but it also can also put you in one. There is something I like to call, "down-stream and up-stream connection." Your downstream connection is to those who need your help, those who look up to you and who glean from you for the purpose of becoming better. Just because you are the down-stream connection, it does

A Beautiful Struggle
Connections Are Everything

---

not mean that you are unbefitting, unworthy of, or less. It just means that you are an apprentice, a disciple or student to the teacher. Your upstream connections are those who can help you. They are your teachers, your mentors and the ones who give you the ability to grow. Without an upstream connection you will always be limited. You will always have the same mindset and you will probably never be challenged to do more or to go higher.

Connection gives you options. When you are connected to different people you have the ability to look at things another way because you get to hear how others look at that same situation. If Jehoshaphat thought like Jehoram, then, most likely, they would have turned around and given up on their journey to pursue promise. But because Jehoshaphat had a different mindset he helped change the mind of Jehoram from blaming to seeking. Jehoshaphat said, Is there not here a prophet of the Lord, that we may enquire of the Lord by him? 2 Kings 3:11

A Beautiful Struggle
Connections Are Everything

    Jehoshaphat's main focus was to seek the Lord for answers. You need to be connected to those who will seek God for solutions in every situation. I do understand that every one that we are connected to is not spiritual, but there should be someone that you are connected to that is. There are many connections that take place in our lives but we always need to be connected to someone that is spiritually minded.

    Jehoshaphat was in a bad predicament because he was connected to Jehoram. So, Jehoshaphat's connection put him in the place of need. The only reason Jehoshaphat was in lack was because of his connection to Jehoram. If you look at where you are right now and you see that you're lacking in a certain area or are in need, you should probably check who you're connected to. If everyone you're connected to is broke, you need new connections. If there is no one connected to you that can help you out of what you're in, whether in word or deed, then you need new connections. Granted, everyone in this world is connected to someone who's in need but you must make sure that you are connected to someone

A Beautiful Struggle
Connections Are Everything

---

that can help meet needs as well. If Jehoshaphat was not connected to Jehoram, everyone would've turned around and given up on the pursuit of promise, but thank God for a good connection. Not only was Jehoshaphat connected to Jehoram, but Jehoshaphat also had connections with a man named Elisha.

Elisha was a prophet of God and the successor of Elijah and he was one of many that accompanied these kings on this journey. The word of the Lord was with Elisha but he was not going to release it because of Jehoram.

Jehoram's lifestyle had a slight resemblance to the lifestyle of his parents and it was evil in the sight of the Lord 2 Kings 3:1-3. Elisha did not agree with his lifestyle and refused to go before the Lord because of Jehoram. 2 Kings 3:13.

Connections are powerful. Elisha refused to cooperate or seek the Lord on behalf of Jehoram, but he did it on behalf of Jehoshaphat. Jehoshaphat was a righteous man and since Jehoshaphat was connected to Jehoram, it says to me that, who you're connected to can help you get things that your character or lifestyle couldn't get you.

Your connection can actually put you in places where you don't deserve to be or shouldn't be or didn't work to be. I remember, many years ago my pastor, Bishop Archie L McInnis, II invited me to an important service. Mind you, I had just started going to Full Effect Gospel Ministries. I was unlearned, unknown and I had never been to an event of this capacity. When we got there they were sitting people and the usher directed me to the back to take a seat. My Bishop turned and said to the usher, "He's sitting with me."

I went to the front and was seated with great leaders and people who had accomplished so much. I was introduced to many people and became friends with some of them. Neither my intellect nor my upbringing brought me to that place. It was simply because of my connection to Bishop McInnis. Many times it's not what you know but whom you know. If you ask any successful person in this world how they got to the place where they are, I can guarantee you that most of them

A Beautiful Struggle
Connections Are Everything

would say that they were connected to someone who helped them.

In Scripture there are so many examples of connections and the results of those connections. Elijah and Elisha were connected. Elisha became great because of Elijah's teaching. Because of this connection, Elisha became the successor of Elijah. Jesus and his disciples were connected, His disciples became apostles at the end because of Jesus' teaching and the relationship that they had with him. Of course, there is a story behind these connections and I'm sure every day wasn't peaches and cream but the point is that your connection is very important. Your connection actually helps shape your future. I believe your friends are your future self. I find this to be true in many instances.

You cannot be connected to or in a relationship with someone for a long period of time and not pick up some of their habits or traits. You can end up sounding like them or even have their mannerisms. The type of people you surround yourself with speaks of your values and what you stand for. We have all heard of the concept of being guilty by association, the act of people associating your behaviors and thoughts with the people you hang out with.

If one of your friends acts negatively, you will be lumped in with him or her. Regardless to whether this is true or not, it is all based on perception. If you believe yourself to be a big-hearted person, a person of discipline, a person with great morals and standards, a time may come when your bad company may start to influence your good behavior. You can be an acquaintance of everyone but you should only be a friend to those who know and serve the Lord as you do.

Don't make the mistake of being connected with bad company, especially when you're working on your future. We all need friends, but we also need the right kind of friends. As a Christian, not any kind of friend will do. Scripture declares in Proverbs 13:20, "He who walks with the wise grow wise, but a companion of fools suffers harm." The point being made in the text is that bad friends lead to bad character. The opposite is also true. Good friends lead to good character. If you have the

A Beautiful Struggle
Connections Are Everything

---

right kind of friends, you will become a better person and a person of wisdom. But if you have the wrong kind of friends, it will cause a lot of trouble and distraction in your life.

You have to be mindful of who you're connected to but mostly understand the strength of your connections. Understanding who acquaintances, associates and who true friends are is very important. Who is the closest to you? Who do you look up to? Who looks up to you? Who's your student? Who's your teacher? Who do you spend the most time with?

In each one of these connections, there is an established system of communication. Whenever there is connection there is communication and wherever there is communication there is influence. The Bible says it like this, "Be not deceived: evil communications corrupt good manners."1 Corinthians 15:33

Let's break this down a little bit. What is the meaning of communication? Communication is a process by which information is exchanged between individuals through a common system of symbols, signs, behavior or language. Evil communication in your connection, whether by symbols, signs, behavior or language, causes a halt in your good way of doing things; it stunts your growth,

It stops your progress. That's why knowing who's around you and who is participating in your life is of upmost importance. Please note that you don't want to get stuck moving and not progressing. You can move and still go nowhere. When you are on a treadmill you are running; you are moving but you are not going anywhere. But when you are progressing there is a forward or onward movement. Your enemy doesn't care if you're moving he just doesn't want you to progress. He understands that if you grow, if you advance and if you progress that you will have the ability to communicate growth, advancement and progression to everyone you are connected to, this will influence them to become better and cause bad manners to become good.

A Beautiful Struggle
Connections Are Everything

We are all connected to someone in some way; let's make sure our connections are helping and not hurting.

CHAPTER FOUR
Worshiping In It

Hard times are unavoidable. They are going to come eventually. No one is exempt from them. No matter how rich you are, no matter how many friends you have, there will be a day when the choices you have made and your responses to God will be tested. When that day comes how will you respond? Will you compromise and despair? Or will you lift your hands and your voice and worship God?

Usually when we speak of worship, the first thing that comes to mind is singing. We start our services with worship and praise music, so that often defines the extent of what we consider to be worship. But worship is defined as reverence offered to a divine being or supernatural power; an act of expressing such reverence; extravagant respect or admiration for or devotion to an object of esteem.

So, worship is so much more than singing and music. It is the life you live as a child of God. It should consume the Christian's life. Worship consists of faith, praise, commitment, confession, prayer, bearing fruit, contentment, and witnessing. All of these are intertwined with worshiping our God and we should not stop operating in them because of what we go through

Job was tested to the core. In one day he lost everything. His property, his herds, his servants and his children were all destroyed in the blink of an eye. Throughout one horrible day Job encountered one tragic story of loss after another. One of the most devastating blows came in the news that all ten of his children had been killed in a windstorm.

Job 1:20-22 tells us how Job responded to the most devastating news anyone could hear. Job stood up and tore his robe in grief. Then he shaved his head and fell to the ground to worship. He said, 'I came naked from my mother's womb, and I will be naked when I leave. The Lord gave me what I had, and the Lord has taken it away. Praise the name of the Lord!" In all of this, Job did not sin by blaming God. Job's response was amazing. In the midst of trouble, he worshipped!

A Beautiful Struggle
Worshiping In It

Notice that Job grieved. He tore his robe and shaved his head. That's what people did in Job's day to express deep grief. He felt the pain but instead of becoming angry or bitter at God because of the pain, he poured the brokenness and the pain out to God through worship.

Job's experience brings up a question: Would you still worship God if everything in your life was going wrong? It's easy to worship when everything is going right. The ultimate test of faith, however, is whether you will still worship in the difficult and painful times. Can you still honor God with extravagant love and extreme submission even when there are hardships in your life? True worship is a matter of the heart expressed through a lifestyle of holiness.

John 4: 23,24 states, "The hour is coming, and is now here, when the true worshipers will worship the Father in spirit and truth, for the Father is seeking such people to worship him. God is spirit, and those who worship him must worship in spirit and truth.

A Beautiful Struggle
Worshiping In It

It is clear that worship is not just doing but worship is being. We have, what I like to call, the act of worship down-packed but the lifestyle of worship is where we fall short.

What is the act of worship? The act of worship is the outward expression of worship.

Through him then let us continually offer up a sacrifice of praise to God, that is, the fruit of lips that acknowledge his name. Do not neglect to do good and to share what you have, for such sacrifices are pleasing to God. Hebrews 13:15-16 ESV

John Piper says, "Through Christ two things become worshipful sacrifices in our life:
the fruit of lips that acknowledge his name [worth]; singing and praying and repenting and confession, and secondly, the fruit of deeds. Don't neglect to do good. Share what you have. Such sacrifices are pleasing to God. "

These are acts of worship. These are the things we do outwardly these are the things we do when we come together on our Sabbath but this is not complete worship. Complete worship is our whole lifestyle of living. Worship is, ultimately, about a whole life – heart, mind, soul, and strength – given over to God, for his use, and joyful service, a life that expresses a high opinion of, and as a result, glorifies God.

Worship is not just what we do, but who we are and what we are about. It should be our life. Worship is the day to day relationship that we have with Christ. This is what Kingdom living was intended to be, and this is true worship; choosing to actively glorify God with your life. So no matter what you go through or what you are up against, worship should always be present in it because you are present in it.

Your response in your toughest seasons will predict the outcome of your victory. Some choose to give up, others make decisions without thinking because of the severity of the situation, but my suggestion for you is to worship in it. Now, some would say that this is easier said than done. One thing I can say is, it is not impossible. I've seen people under extreme hardship in life, still worship God in spite of it. I was at the lowest

A Beautiful Struggle
Worshiping In It

---

part of my life and still worshiped in the midst of it. I was going through a horrible divorce, was faced with financial difficulties to the point that I became homeless, no fault of my own. I lost a lot in that season but I didn't lose my worship. I still gave God what he deserved through worship, both publicly and privately.

I'm talking about daily worship. I would come to church with no money in my pocket and no place to live and give God praise and worship as if everything was alright. I would then leave church and worship him during the week when no one was around. I would sneak away at work or on break and just pray and give thanks. I would walk to my destinations with my headphones on singing and worshipping God. It looked as if I wasn't going through these situations because I worshiped the same way when everything was going well. I WORSHIPED IN IT.

People didn't even realize how much I was dealing with at the time because my worship said "it is well". Your worship has an outside voice. Even when done in private the results of your worship is publicized.

Often times, Jesus would go to a private place where he could be alone to worship God though prayer (Matthew 14:23; Luke 6:12) and the results of this was the preaching and teaching of the gospel to the masses, healing of the sick, deliverance, and people being set free. The worship he gave in private spoke out loud in public through visible results. Once people saw the results, many began to come to see Jesus. Wow! He became famous because of his effectiveness and he was effective because of his private worship. So, the goal shouldn't be to become famous, it should be to become effective.

As you can see in scripture, when you are effective, you become famous (Matthew 4:23-24). We often describe great singers who can exalt and who are used greatly in the spirit as, "real worshippers." But a real worshipper is better determined by what's done in private. How do we handle the things we do when no one is looking? How quickly can we forgive those who have offended us? How do we handle our finances? Do we have integrity? Do we keep our word?

A Beautiful Struggle
Worshiping In It

The scriptures express private actions that yield public rewards very well.

Matthew 6:4-6 KJV says,

That thine alms may be in secret: and thy Father which seeth in secret himself shall reward thee openly. And when thou prayest, thou shalt not be as the hypocrites are: for they love to pray standing in the synagogues and in the corners of the streets, that they may be seen of men. Verily I say unto you, They have their reward. But thou, when thou prayest, enter into thy closet, and when thou hast shut thy door, pray to thy Father which is in secret; and thy Father which seeth in secret shall reward thee openly.

No matter how much you try to explain the pain of what you're going through, no one would ever be able to grasp it because we are all created differently. We are all individuals. We all have different minds but that's why the scripture tells us in Philippians 2:5, "Let this mind be in you, which was also in Christ Jesus." We have to have a Christ-like mindset when it comes to dealing with difficult times and situations.

A Beautiful Struggle
Worshiping In It

Jesus was a worshipper. We can look at many, who worshipped God, but there is only one perfect worshipper and his name is Jesus. He is the model we must follow. His life of intimacy and his daily relationship with God destroyed the works of the devil and his obedience unto death was the ultimate sacrifice that allowed us to be his family of worshippers.

There is a hymn that says, "Daily I shall worship thee Lamb of God Who died for me; Who extended endless mercy; Daily I shall worship thee".

Our worship has to be consistent. A day should not go by without giving God worship. We come together on our Sabbath and we worship him corporately with songs, music and dance but our worship can't stop there. When we leave the church we are also called to worship him in our everyday action. So, it's safe to say our worship on Sunday inspires our worship each day. We honor God with our worship by the way we act among our families, friends, and colleagues. We worship him by offering each and every action to him. So, for example, we worship God by being people who speak the truth from a sincere heart. Surely it's easier to think of worship as something we do for one hour a week in church but worshiping God is an everyday thing. It should be consistent and consistent actions begin with consistent thoughts.

We have all heard the cliché "get your mind right." Javan Rowe states this about worship, "When our thoughts and attitudes are consistent with Scriptural mandates, then our actions will soon be consistent with our beliefs. One of the keys to consistency in our worship, beyond steady progress and attitude, is repetition of prayer and praise. Psalm 119:164 KJV Seven times a day do I praise thee because of thy righteous judgments. I don't think the number here is literal, where as once you reach that number then that's it. The writer is showing repetition in his praise. He is not simply uttering a quick prayer in the morning, but the entire day is lifted up to the Lord. A natural result of always remaining in a state of worship toward the Lord is a peace that is within us that stays. When our lives revolve around the worship of prayer, reading of

A Beautiful Struggle
Worshiping In It

Scripture, and simply praising God, a peace enters that enables us to overcome the obstacles as they come across our path."

So, it's safe to say that worshiping in what we go through helps to keep us from taking drastic actions or making hasty decisions. When you live a life of worship, when things are chaotic, you're at peace, your mind is clearer and you become more sensitive to your environment. Your perception is different and the results of that are the making of wiser decisions and actions.

Worship isn't a place for you to forget your circumstances. It's a place to bring them. It's a place where they find their God-ordained context. Once you make worship the center of your life, whether things are good or bad, you will see different results.

CHAPTER FIVE
Dig Ditches

    I went through a horrific season in my life when everything around me went down.

    So much was going wrong; nothing looked as if it was going to get better.

    I went through a very horrible divorce, and then I was hit with child support that left me with a check for $65 every two weeks. I lost my vehicle because I didn't have the money to maintain it. I lost my apartment so I became homeless for a little while. Some nights I stayed at my mom or my aunt's house. It was very hard to deal with all of these circumstances at once but while I was going through all of this I continued to lead Praise and Worship at my church, I continued to put a smile on my face. I continued to dance, celebrate and worship God. I was in expectation of God bringing me out of what I was in, so I acted as if everything was okay even when it wasn't. I had a good countenance in a bad situation.

A Beautiful Struggle
Dig Ditches

Some would call it faking or putting on a front but I call it digging ditches.

Whenever we come to a point when it looks like all is dry and everything around us is crumbling we tend to either give up or stay where we are. Giving up or staying where we are does not help our situation, it hurts it. Instead of giving up or staying where we are, we need to dig ditches. I define digging ditches as making space for God to pour out blessings in your life.

In 2 Kings 3:16-17 it says," And he said, Thus saith the Lord, Make this valley full of ditches. For thus saith the Lord, Ye shall not see wind, neither shall ye see rain; yet that valley shall be filled with water, that ye may drink, both ye, and your cattle, and your beasts."

The children of Israel had been traveling and came to a place where they were thirsty but there was no water. They were in a very difficult position. Not only were they thirsty but their cattle was thirsty, their beast were thirsty and they were in a valley, A valley is an elongated depression between uplands, hills, or

A Beautiful Struggle
Dig Ditches

mountains; in other words they were at a low point in their situation.

God spoke through Elisha and told them to do something even while they were going through their weak, thirsty, valley situation. He tells them to Dig Ditches! In other words to do two things; have faith and work. He says, believe what He says is going to happen but also do what He says so you can receive what He said.

It doesn't even matter what they were going through; they still had a responsibility to have faith and work the work. But where did God say to have faith? God only said dig ditches. Good question. He said have faith when he told them to dig ditches. You cannot say you believe God if you don't do what he says. Their work in digging ditches said, "I believe what God said will come to pass."

You cannot produce results from God's word if there is no work involved. We all know that faith without works is dead therefore in order to produce results, there needs to be work involved with your faith.

A Beautiful Struggle
Dig Ditches

Not only do you have to believe but you have to do something. The Bible says, "Now faith is the substance of things hoped for the evidence of things not seen." Hebrews 11:1

Let's break this down. Faith is the substance of things hoped for (The word translated "substance" comes from the Greek hupostasis, which means "a placing or setting under, a substructure or foundation.") It is the evidence of things not seen (The word translated, "evidence", comes from the Greek word elengchos, meaning "a proof, or that by which a thing is proved or tested; conviction.") So faith is the foundation and proof of a thing until there is manifestation,

And without it we cannot please God. Hebrews 11:6 You can please God with your faith and still not see the manifestation of what you believe him for. Just because you have faith does not mean what you have faith for will happen. In order to get manifestation of what you believe, works have to be incorporated. Israel

A Beautiful Struggle
Dig Ditches

could have believed what God said and still died of thirst if they didn't do the work of digging.

They had to get dirty. They had to use the little bit of strength they had left to dig ditches. See in order for God to work a miracle in your situation this combination of faith and works has to be implemented. You cannot just believe that God is going to make it better; you have to contribute to the miracle. If there is no contribution with your faith then you leave God no room to work a miracle.

In scripture there are many instances where it took contribution and faith in order for a miracle to be performed. How about the lady with the issue of blood? She pushed through a crowd in order to get to Jesus. She touched the hem of his garment and she was made whole. She believed and did the work. Her work can be seen in her pushing through the crowd.

Let's talk about the four friends who got together and took their crippled friend up on a roof top, tore a hole in the roof and lowered him down to where Jesus was and their friend was healed. Along with their faith,

A Beautiful Struggle
Dig Ditches

they climbed up on a roof and tore a hole in it and the lowered him down, that was work. Just because you are going through a difficult situation does not give you the okay to stop working. The enemy wants you to stop doing what you are doing because he understands there is power in your work. He understands when others see that you refuse to stop in spite of all that you are going through they become encouraged, they become empowered, they begin to say, if he can do it then I can do it, too. You become a living epistle. You become undeniable proof that if you use your faith and work the work, things will turn around in your favor.

Digging ditches while you're going through says you believe the word that God has spoken. You are working with no proof or details of how the situation is going to get better; all you have is his word telling you to dig. So now you can understand that it's not faking and it's not fronting, its digging. I'm smiling even though I should be crying; I'm digging. I'm showing love even though I'm not receiving it from the ones that I want to receive it from; I'm digging. I'm still going to church, I'm

A Beautiful Struggle
Dig Ditches

---

still going to work, I'm still taking care of my family; I am digging. When depression and suicidal thoughts come to your mind and you fight them with prayer and fasting that's work, you're digging.

I want to pause for a moment to encourage you. Whatever you do, don't stop digging. Keep doing the work. Keep believing because you will see the manifestation of what you've been believing and working on.

The beautiful thing about faith and works is that you will always get the best results in the end. People won't understand how you made it through all you've experienced.

Let us not forget that Israel's obedience played a part also with faith and works. God loves it when you do what he says. God has no other choice but to provide when you obey. Use your faith and work.

Obedience is powerful. Look what the scripture says about obedience.

Deuteronomy 28:1-14 NIV

A Beautiful Struggle
Dig Ditches

---

1 If you fully obey the Lord your God and carefully follow all his commands I give you today, the Lord your God will set you high above all the nations on earth. 2 All these blessings will come on you and accompany you if you obey the Lord your God:

3 You will be blessed in the city and blessed in the country.

4 The fruit of your womb will be blessed, and the crops of your land and the young of your livestock—the calves of your herds and the lambs of your flocks.

5 Your basket and your kneading trough will be blessed.

6 You will be blessed when you come in and blessed when you go out.

7 The Lord will grant that the enemies who rise up against you will be defeated before you. They will come at you from one direction but flee from you in seven.

8 The Lord will send a blessing on your barns and on everything you put your hand to. The Lord your God will bless you in the land he is giving you.

A Beautiful Struggle
Dig Ditches

---

9 The Lord will establish you as his holy people, as he promised you on oath, if you keep the commands of the Lord your God and walk in obedience to him.

10 Then all the peoples on earth will see that you are called by the name of the Lord, and they will fear you.

11 The Lord will grant you abundant prosperity—in the fruit of your womb, the young of your livestock and the crops of your ground—in the land he swore to your ancestors to give you.

12 The Lord will open the heavens, the storehouse of his bounty, to send rain on your land in season and to bless all the work of your hands. You will lend to many nations but will borrow from none.

13 The Lord will make you the head, not the tail. If you pay attention to the commands of the Lord your God that I give you this day and carefully follow them, you will always be at the top, never at the bottom.

14 Do not turn aside from any of the commands I give you today, to the right or to the left, following other gods and serving them.

A Beautiful Struggle
Dig Ditches

When obedience is implemented, God makes sure he takes care of you. That's why it is always good to obey God rather than to disobey. Even if what he is asking you to do is weird or unusual, it is best that you do it because your win is guaranteed when you obey. When we obey God, we will never be disappointed. Israel's survival depended on their obedience, their faith and their work. You'll survive if you obey, have faith and do the work.

Do what God said, believe that what he says will come to pass and then keep functioning and working as if it's already done. All of this makes room for God to show up on your behalf. It gets tough and sometimes it will be hard but knowing that the outcome will be victorious and beautiful gives you the strength to be consistent. The consistency of your obedience, faith and works should be priority. Anything you do consistently will become habitual. If you make it a habit to be obedient to God, have faith and to work the works of God then you will always win.

CHAPTER SIX
Results After Offering

The giving of offering is a spiritual issue and in fact, a relational issue with God. When we say God is our father we are speaking about a relationship that we have with him. We can let everyone know that what he has is ours what we have is his.

Once you understand the Father gave you everything that you have you won't have a problem giving offerings to him. You must not only offer God material things but spiritual things as well. Your offering is just not your money but it is your life. It is your work. It is what you give to what you believe in or respect. What you are offering and to whom you are offering it says a lot about what or who you love.

Matthew 6:21 says, "For where your treasure is, there will your heart be also." Even though our life is consumed with offering things to people and offering things in exchange for things, nothing is more important than giving offerings to God. Whether you know it or not, offerings bring forth results dependent upon how you give.

The Scripture says "But this I say, He which soweth sparingly shall reap also sparingly; and he which soweth bountifully shall reap also bountifully." What you offer to God and how you offer it is totally up to you. Granted a lot of people don't have a problem giving their life as an offering to God or giving their labor as an offering to God but many people do have a problem giving their money as an offering to God.

When talking about giving money to God we must deal with two things; tithe and offering. Offerings are different from the tithe; God requires the tithe as an act of obedience in a Christian's life. The offering is an act of our free will. We make something valuable enough to give into it or support it with our free will funds. God gives us the ability to make, acquire and control money in our lives. The topic of offerings and tithe or rather money and church tends to be avoided a lot of times. Some consider it to be one of the most dreaded and uncomfortable topics both to preach and to

A Beautiful Struggle
Results After Offering

hear about. Money and giving can stir all kinds of emotions and reactions in even the most faithful Christians.

Although I understand the urge to avoid this conversation, Jesus modeled talking about this important issue more than any other. The Bible has a lot to say about money. It's closely tied to our hearts, to our relationship with Jesus, and to the work he's called us to do. Jesus said money is the primary competitor for Lordship in our lives. He said, "You cannot serve God and money" (Matt. 6:24). He actually didn't say this about any other issue. So, giving money to God says that he is the ultimate Lord of my life. The other thing about giving offerings to God is that it guarantees you results. Whenever there's an offering there are results. Let's look at some scriptures.

2 Kings 3:20 KJV says, "And it came to pass in the morning, when the meat offering was offered, that, behold, there came water by the way of Edom, and the country was filled with water."

A Beautiful Struggle
Results After Offering

Israel received their results after they gave their meeting's offering. Their results were water. The meat offering wasn't an offering of meat; it's originally a gift of any kind. The Hebrew denotes an "unbloody" sacrifice, as opposed to a "bloody" sacrifice. Once they offered it water came. Water was what they needed and what they asked for because they were on a journey in pursuit of promise and they received it once they gave an offering.

Your offering causes God to move on your behalf because it is a sign of worship and faith. Our offerings are an act of worship. The offering provides believers the opportunity to respond in gratitude to the grace, love, and mercy of God and to put their faith and trust in the Lord into action. Our offering to God is an act of worship just like singing hymns, hearing a sermon, and engaging in prayer. It is also faith in action. Giving offerings or better yet sowing seed takes faith. When you do this it brings God glory. When you sow, you will always reap. Jesus described this principle of sowing and reaping when he was trying to explain why he came to

A Beautiful Struggle
Results After Offering

Earth to die on the cross. "Verily, verily, I say unto you, Except a corn of wheat fall into the ground and die, it abideth alone: but if it die, it bringeth forth much fruit." John 12:24 KJV Jesus was simply saying that millions of people will be saved and go to heaven because of his death and resurrection. He was going to plant a seed, and that seed was his life.

The principle of sowing and reaping is planting a seed wherever you have a need. Whatever it is you need; more time, more energy, more money, more support, more relationships, more wisdom, just plant a seed. If you need more time, give more time to your kids. If you need more money, give it away to someone who needs it. If you need more wisdom, share what wisdom you have with others. Give yourself away!

It is good for us to learn to give. When we give something to someone, we are showing love, respect and concern for that person. The offering, as it passes between the giver and the receiver represents a bond of affection between the two parties. In this case, it's us and God. I love God so much that I'm willing to give him anything and everything. Just like he loved us so much that he gave his only begotten son.

When we follow the principles the Lord gives us, we will find that we need less miracles. Giving and sowing seed is a principle. It is guaranteed to work if you work it. The principle applies to everyone, both Christians and non-Christians. This principle is not racist or bias it is set. It cannot be revoked or reversed there is no escape for the Believer or for the Unbeliever. It is a law of life. Galatians 6:7 says, "Be not deceived; God is not mocked: for whatsoever a man soweth, that shall he also reap." It says, Do not be deceived, God is not mocked. Anyone who does not sow or does not believe in sowing are the deceived. They either do not believe the truth, or they think they will somehow be the exceptions to God's laws

It is a spiritual law, as powerful and as dependable as any natural law. Luke 6:38 says, Give, and it shall be given unto you; good measure, pressed down, and shaken together, and running over, shall men give into your bosom. For with the same measure that ye

A Beautiful Struggle
Results After Offering

---

mete withal [measure] it shall be measured to you again." You see, God has guaranteed that a gift always comes back, in good measure, pressed down, shaken together, and running over. Whatever you sow, you will reap.

I didn't always believe in sowing. It was a struggle for me to put out money and I had unpaid bills. If the truth be told the money I had wasn't enough to pay the bills anyway but because I was ignorant of the principle of sowing and reaping, I still didn't sow seed or tithe and that was a big mistake.

Nothing that I did worked. No matter how hard I tried it all failed. I was recycling my poverty. I was on welfare; not just on it for help but I depended on it. I wasn't able to keep a job more than a year. I was always broke; always asking someone for help or money; nothing worked.

My Bishop released me from everything I was doing in ministry. He prayed with me and taught me the principles of sowing. He showed me that I was preventing God from blessing me. After a while I began

A Beautiful Struggle
Results After Offering

---

to see the results of sowing seed. I went from depending on welfare to maintaining a financial flow. I was able to land a steady job that was paying well. I was consistent at that job and worked there for over 10 years. Things began to work and turn in my favor. I'm so glad I started sowing seed because it brought forth results.

Giving always results in receiving. L*uke 6:38 says:* Give, and it shall be given unto you; good measure, pressed down, and shaken together, and running over, shall men give into your bosom. For with the same measure that ye mete withal [measure] it shall be measured to you again." When you become a giver, you automatically move yourself into the realm of a receiver. There are no exceptions to this rule. By the world's principles of economics, when you give something away, you then have less. If you give away money or land or food that leaves you with less of the thing you have given away. But that is not the case according to God's principles. He teaches that when you give something away it always ends up returning to you, multiplied. You cannot lose ground; you only gain it by

A Beautiful Struggle
Results After Offering

---

giving to God. Deuteronomy 8:18; NKJV says, "And you shall remember the Lord your God, for it is He who gives you power to get wealth."

In order for you to get wealth there has to be some giving involved. Your gift is a natural key that unleashes a supernatural miracle working force in your life. Giving always prospers you.

CHAPTER SEVEN
Not Just Water

God loves to bless us with more than what we need. He loves us so much that he would even give us things that we didn't ask for. When you look back over your life you can think of many occasions where God showed up and blessed you with more abundantly.

I've experienced this so many times in my life. When I asked God to get me through a difficult situation and when I look back, he got me through it and gave me extra in it. I asked for just enough when God wanted me to have more than enough.

In 2 Kings 3, the king of Israel, the king of Judah, and the king of Edom ran into a situation where they needed water. If they did not receive water they would not survive the journey. They inquired of the Lord through the prophet Elisha and God spoke through him and gave them specific instructions to dig ditches. This is all in Chapter 3 of 2 Kings, but I want to point out something very interesting. In response to their

A Beautiful Struggle
Not Just Water

---

obedience, the Lord did not just give them what they needed which was water but he gave them much more.

Let's look at 2 Kings 3:17-10

For thus saith the Lord, Ye shall not see wind, neither shall ye see rain; yet that valley shall be filled with water, that ye may drink, both ye, and your cattle, and your beasts. And this is but a light thing in the sight of the Lord: he will deliver the Moabites also into your hand. And ye shall smite every fenced city, and every choice city, and shall fell every good tree, and stop all wells of water, and mar every good piece of land with stones.

God did not just give them just water; he gave them territory, the victory over their enemies, and he even gave them control over what they needed because he said they would have the ability to stop all wells of water.

What they once lacked God gave them control over. Now that's way more than what they asked for. They just wanted to survive the journey but God wanted them to have more. I believe in my heart that God wants his children to have more than just water for survival. He wants us to have pleasure, too. Many of us today are living in survival mode. If we can just make it through the day, we've accomplished our goal. There are times when circumstances can seem overwhelming and there are seasons that are more difficult than others but God doesn't want us to just survive,

God wants us to thrive. He wants us to prosper in all things. You don't have to settle for an average year; you can have an extraordinary year. I get it. Life is hard. It's easy to become bitter and grumble through your situation. Whether it's your job or maybe your marriage is on the rocks, or you don't know how you are going to pay your rent. You may have recently lost someone you love. No matter what you are going through, God didn't create you to just barely make it. He didn't create you to spend time wasting your days in doubt and feeling sorry for yourself. God desires for you to thrive. He wants you to live an abundant life. He has a specific purpose for each and every day you face and He has created you to live your life to the fullest. He encourages you to thrive

A Beautiful Struggle
Not Just Water

through every day and yes that includes thriving even when you are in the middle of a difficult trial.

Stop settling for less than what the Lord has already paid for. Because of what Jesus did on the cross, you get to live in complete victory. There are two people who will prevent a bountiful life from manifesting and they are the enemy and yourself. Make a decision today to thrive through the abundant life God has set out before you. You have the power to choose.

One other thing I recognize in the Scripture is that they received more than water because they followed God's instructions. He told them to dig ditches. In spite of everything they were going through; they were tired because of the journey, they were thirsty, they were hot and they were in a valley. All of these things were taking place and God still wanted them to dig ditches.

You see God needed them to do something in order for him to do what he promised and that something was to obey. He needed them to obey, because their obedience showed trust. The Scripture says obedience is better than sacrifice. When you obey his instructions and do what he says, it shows that you trust God. You allow God to give you more when you trust him. I find that it is easy to trust in God's deliverance but not as easy to follow God's instruction.

Proverbs 16:20 NLT states that, "Those who listen to instruction will prosper; those who trust the LORD will be joyful." You can choose to go about things your own way, but if you do, then the promises are not guaranteed.

The Scripture says we will prosper when we follow instructions but for some reason we still find it very difficult to do so, whether it be because of sacrifices that need to be made or maybe a relationship that needs to be severed. Sometimes difficult decisions have to be made when following the instructions of God. This is where your trust and faith comes into the picture.

Faith and obedience are interlocked. God has linked faith and obedience together so that all of the promises of God are conditioned upon you following the directions that He gives you. If God tells you to do

A Beautiful Struggle
Not Just Water

something believe me he has your back. He always makes sure that you he provides you with what you need and much more. Applying faith and obedience to His commands in our lives is the key to experiencing the presence of Christ and the joy of heaven. Jesus says, the one who obeys him is the one who loves him...He will only reveal himself to those who love him and obey him. It took Israel's faith and obedience to receive water from nowhere.

    The Bible says, "For thus saith the Lord, Ye shall not see wind, neither shall ye see rain; yet that valley shall be filled with water, that ye may drink, both ye, and your cattle, and your beasts." 2 Kings 3:17. God told them what to do (dig ditches) and in return he would give them what they needed (water). What they needed didn't come the way it usually would with gray clouds, strong winds and heavy rain. God didn't need any of that to give them what they needed. He gave it to them out of nowhere.

    That's amazing! God can bless you out of nowhere. What doesn't exist, God can make exist.

A Beautiful Struggle
Not Just Water

Where there is no way he can create a way. If you activate your faith and obey God's word he has a way of making things happen without the necessities.

Sometimes we think we can't accomplish our goals because of the things we don't have. We tend to quit before we finish because we are focused on the things we lack, but when you have faith in God and you listen and obey his word, God can make things happen even when you don't have the necessary requirements. Mary the mother of Jesus is an example; she asked how she could give birth to a child when she was a virgin. We all know what it takes to become pregnant and conceive. A man and woman is what it takes to produce a baby but the angel told her the Holy Spirit will come upon you, and the power of the Most High will overshadow you and you will give birth to a baby boy. She did not need what she thought she needed in order to give birth to a child. God did it! He went against the natural process of reproduction and did it his own way. God doesn't need assistance when it comes to blessing you. He is God, He can do all things. But he does want your obedience. Let's get back to that for a minute.

Obedience is what causes God to send water without rain. So it's safe to say that God responds to obedience. When you choose to obey the Lord, He will bless you. Obedience *always* leads to blessing. Very often, God's greatest blessings come as a result of our willingness to do something that appears very insignificant or difficult.

So ask yourself, has God been challenging me to do some things that seem unimportant that I have not yet made an effort to accomplish? Is there anything I have put off from doing because I said it's too difficult? I don't want to do it or I have to pray about it first? God wants your obedience so he can bless you out of nowhere. I don't care what you are going through or what you are up against; there is a way out and that way out is through the obedience of God.

God always has a way of making things work in your life and giving you more than what you expected. Take time out to talk to him and hear what he has to say then do what he says and watch how things turn around in your favor.

You will see results. You may not see the details of it, you may not understand how it was done but one day you will look back and say, "God did it and he gave me more than what I expected." That's the beauty of the struggle when God is with us. We are never alone and He gives us more in the end. He turns our trials into trophies. What we thought was going to get the best of us, truly made the best out of us.

www.ingramcontent.com/pod-product-compliance
Lightning Source LLC
LaVergne TN
LVHW051510070426
835507LV00022B/3034